7/10

COLLEGE ADMISSION 101:

A Guide for Homeschooling Families

RUTH COUSINS

CROSS

BOOKS

CrossBooks™
1663 Liberty Drive
Bloomington, IN 47403
www.crossbooks.com
Phone: 1-866-879-0502

First published by CrossBooks 02/03/10

ISBN: 978-1-6150-7085-5 (sc)

Library of Congress Control Number: 2009941230

Printed in the United States of America
Bloomington, Indiana

This book is printed on acid-free paper.

This book is dedicated to my husband John and to my children who taught me volumes everyday. I also want to thank my favorite English teacher Jean Belz who taught a recalcitrant child to love the written word.

Contents

INTRODUCTION

Sending your homeschooled student off to college can be an overwhelming idea! After all you have diligently guided your little darling through so many texts and workbooks that you may not have seen the dining room table for years. You have been their teacher, principal and guidance counselor. Now you are contemplating, with a certain amount of angst, the idea of foisting them onto an unsuspecting public. I know, I've been there! On the one hand, you may feel ready to move on to other activities like regular showers and coffee with friends. On the other hand, passing the educational baton is a momentous occasion. After homeschooling your adolescent, climbing Mt. Everest, or planning the invasion of a small country, should be well within your abilities. Just as you have overcome the many hurdles of a home educator, I have full confidence that you will also be able to navigate the confusing world of College Admissions. This book was born out my own feeble struggles to help my student select appropriate colleges, investigate them and then present her academic and other accomplishments. After all, your student's information will be deposited onto the desk of a very overworked and overwhelmed admissions official. You must use this brief window to help your student put their best foot forward.

I soon became aware that the high school years would be a series of dates. Dates for testing, dates for applications and of course dates for scholarships. I looked in vain for a manual that would walk me through this process. While I found some help with transcripts, there was nothing that explained how the admissions system worked or the importance of paying attention to dates and a time line.

The goal of this publication is to give you some tools to help you organize your search, plan a college preparatory curriculum, gather your documentation and finally to create a group of documents to present your student for admission. I have used the experiences I gained over a four year process to streamline this process for you. Many of these things you may already know but I hope you will benefit from having this reference to help you on your journey. Were we successful? Well you be the judge. Our student was accepted to every institution to which she applied. She was offered Presidential Scholarships at three Universities and eventually accepted an offer at her first choice. At this point some of you will cast this book aside thinking it was only written for students who are performing in the top percentile. While it is true that much of the content is geared to achieving the best results for those students, I think it is important for any student contemplating college to present themselves in the best way possible. Friends and relatives who home school asked to see the "Admission Packet" that we compiled, and many asked to borrow from it. But the "Admission Packet" was only one part of this process. Like everything else in homeschooling, the process of finding and applying to a university requires lots of work and commitment. I have attempted with this manual to walk you through it step by step. Many of these steps will seem self explanatory, if so, congratulations! You're half way there. To others all of these concepts may seem completely overwhelming.If you are one of these, just take courage from how scary it was to begin homeschooling your precious babies! You succeeded with that, and you can succeed at finding them a college that will be a great fit for the next step in their education. So, as you begin here at the Base Camp gather your equipment and your fortitude and before you know it the Summit will be in you and your students' sights!

CHAPTER I

Curriculum

If you have picked up this book at the most optimal time, then your student is about to enter the first year of their High School Curriculum. I say this because you will be able to reap the most benefit from this book with the least amount of stress. If your student is a senior you may still be able to benefit but you may also be tearing your hair out in trying to accomplish all of the things necessary. So I will begin with what is usually referred to as the freshman year.

Before your students freshman year you should sit down with their list of classes to date. Some of you will have students that have already taken courses that are normally considered high school level. I remember standing in line at a home school convention behind parents who were trying to pick a Pre-Calculus course for their thirteen year old daughter. Yikes! Of course both parents were Engineers so that made me feel a little better. This digression was merely to illustrate that I know there are genius children among us. If one of those precocious youngsters is yours, you will need to carry over all appropriate credits onto the High School Transcript. I will discuss this in more depth when I discuss the High School Transcript in a subsequent chapter.

Most Colleges and Universities require three to four units of English. That means three to four full years of courses that include Literature, Writing or Journalism, and of course Grammar. As a homeschooling family you have the flexibility to do a full year of curriculum in a much shorter time period. Generally a good rule of thumb is three hours a week times 36 weeks. This can be counted as a year of curriculum or one full unit. So if your student can put in nine hours a week, a course can be completed in twelve weeks. As you will see, whenever you do something unorthodox with your curriculum you must document it fully. One of the curriculum ideas I highly recommend, is that your student use of some type of vocabulary builder. For instance, anything that focuses on the Latin or Greek roots of the English language will be very beneficial when it comes time for standardized testing. Also, even though Analogies are no longer a separate part of the SAT or ACT tests, they are still very beneficial for critical thinking and logical analysis. I also recommend that you make writing a daily occurrence. Start your student on a path that includes several research papers every year. Invest in a manual that details the ALA or MLA writing requirements. Different college classes will require different types of annotation. Having a manual that shows several styles will acquaint your student with these different requirements. These are usually available at bookstores. I also cannot emphasize enough the value of Classic Literature. They are great for building vocabulary and reading comprehension. Introduce your student to the Last of the Mohicans or that rascal Heathcliff. They are much more enriching than whatever is on their Facebook page.

The minimum requirements for High School Math are generally Algebra I, II and Geometry. However this is only the minimum and I recommend that you have completed these before the fall of their junior year. In fact, the more higher level math your student can have completed before this, the better their chances are of a high score on the PSAT test. If you have a student that you feel may have the propensity to score in the top ten percent on national testing, you will want to set up a curriculum that will take them through Pre-Calculus before they take this test. The PSAT is given in the fall of their junior year. For instance, you may want your student to take Algebra I first semester, Algebra II second semester of their freshman year and Geometry during the summer or the first semester of the sophomore year. Then you can use the second semester, or even the summer to get good start on Pre-Calculus. Any courses after this would be dependent on your students' interests. Calculus would be appropriate if they have interests in Mathematics, Engineering or Science. Weighting these courses so early in the high school years may seem intimidating for both you and your student. If there was not such a wealth of excellent Math curriculum I would agree. However Math curriculum has come a long way since those of us who struggled through Algebra I left high school. One of the strengths of home schooling is that we have many options in curriculum for different learning styles. If your child gets stuck, and you as parents get stuck, think about hiring a local college student as a tutor. If it fits your budget it will be a blessing to the tutor and give your overworked intellect a break!

Most Universities and Colleges like to see at least two Laboratory Science Courses on your students' transcript. Three courses that include a lab component are generally required for scholarship consideration. At a minimum they should have taken both Biology and Chemistry. Physics is also highly recommended. As always documentation is your friend. Keep track of lab hours and reflect them in your course description. Science Camps at local universities can be used for lab hours also and reflect your students desire to learn and go beyond basic requirements. Science curriculum is always a challenge for families that have very firm convictions in regard to the Origins of the Universe. You may be wondering why anyone would voluntarily send their student to a Science Camp where, in all likelihood, they will be exposed to a very secular world view. This reasonable objection will have to be carefully weighed within your own family as to its benefits verses its risk.

Sadly, History and other Social Sciences are the poor cousins of college requirements. Most institutions only require two of these units. So this is my opportunity to wax eloquent on behalf of Historical Literacy. Can we in good conscience allow our students to matriculate without a firm grounding in World and U.S. history? At a minimum I would like to see all students take a World History Course that stresses the value of Western Civilization and a complete History of the United States, including familiarity with our founding documents. A good curriculum should also include a course on U.S. Government and Economics. Once these basics have been taken, your student may want to explore courses in Psychology or Sociology. If your student is working through a basic college level text they should be able to take a test at the end of their course of study and obtain college credit for these courses. This can save your student several thousand dollars once they begin their college career. I will go into a discussion on CLEP and

3

AP credits in a subsequent chapter, if you're dying of curiosity I give you permissions to skip ahead.

Usually two years of the same foreign language are required for consideration for admission. You may be thinking that given the trend toward more Spanish speakers in the U.S. that this would be your first choice as a foreign language. If your family is already bilingual, bravo! Your student is already far ahead of the rest of his peers. While Spanish is a lovely and lyrical language I would like you to think about having your student start with Latin I and II instead. "Ridiculous!" you say. "The bicycle assembly instructions are never printed in Latin but are almost always printed in English, Spanish and maybe Urdu!" While all of this is true I would like to bring to your attention the fact that all curriculum before the epical 1960's included Latin. Why, you ask? It's because it is generally acknowledged that most of our own language, and all Romance Languages (i.e. Spanish, French and Portuguese) were direct descendants of Latin. Studying Latin also trains your youngsters mind to learn other languages. Wrestling with conjugations, declensions and vocabulary prepares them to build their English language skills and makes other languages easier to learn.

Now that you have the basics down, it is time to think about Electives. These are classes that are not part of any requirement but instead give the folks in Admissions an idea about the things your student has studied and enjoyed beyond academic requirements. These include any type of Musical Performance or Art. It may also include thing like Computer courses or even Agriculture or Horticulture. Admissions faculty see many students with great grades and impressive lists of courses. They also like to see students who enjoy things outside what is strictly required. If your student wants to take a course in Child Development by all means include it in your curriculum. Choose classes in which your student has an interest or even better, a passion. Anything that captures your students' imagination can be developed into a course; even dare I say it, Video Game Design!

Now you are probably scratching your head and wondering how, at this early stage, can we decide on every course for the next four years? What I have given you is a basic skeleton which you must now embellish based on your own students' aptitudes and desires. And, the best thing is, because you home school, you have the flexibility to add, delete, or change directions midstream. If you already have an institution in mind, I would also urge you to contact them or visit their website to find their exact requirements. While I have given you a general idea of requirements, each institution sets its own standards. These can even vary within institutions based on individual majors. For instance a student who plans on a career in Engineering will need more advanced Math and Science than a Liberal Arts Major. It is never too early to investigate the particulars of any college in which your student may be interested.

As with most successful endeavors thoughtful planning will allow you to proceed with a goal in mind. If four years of planning seems too overwhelming to your student it may be helpful to remind them that they really only need to focus on the task at hand. Responsibility for an overall plan falls to the parent wearing many hats. That right it's you!

SUMMARY

PLAN YOUR CURRICULUM EARLY
INCLUDE:

-MATHEMATICS (ALGEBRA I&II, GEOMETRY, AND POSSIBLY PRE-CALCULUS AND CALCULUS.

-ENGLISH (FOUR YEARS INCLUDING LITERATURE, WRITING, GRAMMAR, AND VOCABULARY).

-SCIENCE (THREE YEARS OF GENERAL OR EARTH SCIENCE, BIOLOGY, CHEMISTRY, AND POSSIBLY PHYSIC)*NOTE LABS.

-HISTORY (TWO YEARS MINIMUM, WORLD AND UNITED STATES, AND GOVERNMENT/ECONOMICS).

-FOREIGN LANGUAGE (TWO YEARS, CONSIDER LATIN I&II)

-ELECTIVES (MUSIC, ART, AGRICULTURE ETC.).

REMEMBER YOU CAN RE-ADJUST THIS AS YOUR STUDENT PROGRESSES THROUGH THE CURRICULUM.

CHAPTER II

Deciphering Standardized Tests

Because homeschooled students receive most, if not all, of their grades from their parents, colleges place extra weight on the results of standardized testing. For example, if your little darlings' transcript reflects a GPA of 4.0, admission personal will expect to see scores close to the top ten percentile. But you may say, "Billy has never done well on standardized tests!" While this may be true, and we all know bright students who have a great deal of difficulty taking timed tests, you will be hard pressed to convince anyone that your student deserves consideration over others whose transcripts and testing are consistent. There are ways to improve test performance and it may be worth the time and effort to pursue these. One of simplest is merely to take the tests as frequently as you can. It has long been thought that one of the reasons students in Iowa generally test at the top nationally is because they start taking the Iowa Test of Basic Skills at a very young age. By the time those students are in Middle School they have taken these tests so many times that test taking anxiety is greatly reduced. If your child has a disability you may also ask for accommodations appropriate to that disability.

As I mentioned in the previous chapter you may find it helpful to enlist the aid of tutors to improve specific areas. There are many Study Guides available at bookstores and even libraries to help students prepare for these tests. There are also classes available at Public Schools and even Online that can help your student focus on improving test scores. I would also suggest that you schedule time in your students' day specifically to study for standardized testing. I was quite surprised to find out, from a friend whose daughter applied to Harvard, that many of the elite prep schools in our country spend a considerable amount of time schooling their students in order to get perfect scores on both ACT and SAT tests. Their goal is to get most of their graduates into Ivy League Universities where a perfect score is the norm. Living in rural Iowa I searched the Internet to find a class in our remote area that helped improve my students' score by ten percent. While the class she attended emphasized learning to eliminate wrong answers and deduct the likely answer, we also concurrently focused on reading literature classics, the Wall Street Journal, and The Federalist Papers. We also spent a great deal of time looking over previous test scores and emphasized areas where testing had shown weakness.

The first Standardized test I will discuss is the PSAT/NMSQT. This test is given in the fall of your students' Junior Year and is used to evaluate students for National Merit Scholarships. It also is a means of collecting information on your students' interests and abilities for a variety of programs. Your student may take this test before their junior year and I would recommend that they do so. Taking the test early will give you valuable information on where you need to focus your efforts academically. None of the scores earned before the junior year will count either for or against the scores obtained in their junior year, but taking the test early can give you very valuable information, as well as letting your student have firsthand experience with this particular testing style. There are three tests subjects; they include Critical Reading, Mathematics, and Writing Skills.Scores range from 20-80. Students with the highest test scores in their state will then take an additional test as a National Merit Semifinalist, and subsequently as a National Merit Finalist. Even if your student is not selected to continue on as a Semifinalist their scores, even in the 80th percentile, will open up many educational opportunities. There are registration deadlines for this test and you should be able to get enrollment information from your local public school or Online. I recommend that you contact them to get this information in August of your students' Junior Year or you may take a "practice" PSAT in the autumn of your Sophomore Year.

The Stanford Achievement Test, or SAT, is given several times in the fall and spring. This test also includes sections on Critical Reading, Mathematics and Writing Skills. The tests scores are between 200-800. Most of the colleges we dealt with really only consider the Critical Reading and Mathematics sections. The jury is still out on the accuracy of the section on Writing Skills and so many schools don't factor those scores into consideration. You may obtain more information on both the PSAT and the SAT by logging onto **www.collegeboard.com**. If your student takes this test more than once, some colleges will pick the best scores from each test. Other colleges will only consider each test event individually. Again these are specific questions that should be posed to the individual universities your student is considering. Your student may begin to take the SAT test early and it is in their best interest to do so their junior year. Scores earned before this time will not be relevant to admission but are beneficial in familiarizing your student with the style of this particular test. Again, I will mention that ordering a report after the test scores have been received, will allow you and your student to evaluate your current curriculum.

The other choice for college entrance exams is the ACT test. This test is also given several times in the spring and autumn across the U.S. It is widely available through your local public school and is accepted by most Colleges and Universities. This test involves English, Mathematics, Reading, Science, and has an optional Writing Component. The top score for each test is 36. The test scores are averaged in order to obtain a Composite Score. Preparatory classes for this test are available through many sources, especially in the Midwestern States. You may want to have your student take both the SAT and the ACT tests as many students will do better on one style of test than the other.

Subject Tests are standardized tests that are required by many of your top universities. The tests will focus on the depth and breadth of your students' knowledge in individual core subjects. You can obtain more information on Subject Tests by visiting **www.collegeboard.com** or by visiting the Test Prep section of a large bookstore. Most students will not need to take any of these subject tests. However, if your student has their heart set on Dartmouth or Princeton, you will probably need to access this information.

Another type of standardized test that I will discuss is CLEP or AP tests. These are given to assess your students' knowledge in specific subjects in order to earn College Credit. In the chapter on curriculum I made reference to the subjects of Psychology and Sociology. These are two subjects that are frequently CLEP'ed. Since every University has its own list of classes that they will allow their students to CLEP, you must investigate this carefully before you pay and prepare for individual tests. Also caution must be exercised when accumulating CLEP credits. If you enter college with more than 20 CLEP credits your student may not be considered a freshman and may be ineligible for many scholarships. CLEP tests may be taken on a monthly basis at most area Community Colleges. The credits will then be sent to the college of your choice. AP or Advanced Placement tests are usually given once a year in early May. Sign up for these tests is late winter and they may be taken through your local school district or other testing centers. AP classes show admissions personnel that your student has gone beyond basic requirements and is willing to put in the extra effort of a more demanding class regimen.

In summary I will reiterate, start taking standardized tests early to reduce anxiety and provide you with valuable information on your students relative strengths and weaknesses. Take both the SAT and ACT if possible in order to find out if your student prefers one testing style over the other. Try to take the PSAT before the junior year in order become familiar with the subjects and style of the test. Try to schedule time within your school day to study for testing. It can easily be used as part of your Vocabulary, Reading and Writing Competence and even review of Math skills. If you feel your student would benefit from more intensive preparation, investigate classes offered in your area. When it comes to obtaining CLEP or AP credits, make sure the institutions you are looking at will accept the test your student is planning on taking.

A final note of caution would be that you and your student should not be discouraged if the initial test results are not exemplary. Remember, the first time you dip your toe into the pool it's bound to be rather shocking. Don't let this discourage you from continuing your swim. Eventually what is difficult can become fun, if you and your student are willing to put in the time and effort.

SUMMARY

PSAT: PRELIMINARY STANFORD ACHIEVEMENT TEST, THE TEST TAKEN IN YOUR STUDENTS JUNIOR YEAR. THIS TEST IS A QUALIFIER FOR CONSIDERATION FOR NATIONAL MERIT SCHOLARSHIP QUALIFYING TEST OR NMSQT.

SAT: STANFORD ACHIEVEMENT TEST, ONE OF THE COLLEGE ENTRANCE EXAMS REQUIRED FOR ADMISSION.

ACT: AMERICAN COLLEGE TEST, ANOTHER OF THE COLLEGE ENTRANCE TESTS ACCEPTED BY MOST INSTITUTIONS.

CLEP: COLLEGE LEVEL EXAMINATION PROGRAM, TESTING THAT WILL QUALIFY YOUR STUDENT TO RECEIVE COLLEGE CREDITS BY TESTING IN INDIVIDUAL SUBJECTS.

ADVANCED PLACEMENT: TESTING THAT IS DONE AFTER YOUR STUDENT HAS COMPLETED A COLLEGE LEVEL COURSE IN THEIR HIGH SCHOOL CURRICULUM SO THAT COLLEGE CREDITS CAN BE AWARDED.

SUBJECT TESTS: TESTING THAT IS REQUIRED BY HIGHLY SELECTIVE UNIVERSITIES ON INDIVIDUAL SUBJECTS PRIOR TO AN ADMISSION DECISION.

CHAPTER III

The College Search

Depending on how far along in their high school career your student may be, you might consider it premature to be evaluating different colleges. On the other hand you may feel very strongly that your child attend your Alma Mater and have already invested resources to that end. If that is the case you may skip this chapter entirely! As for those of you who think the freshman year is too early to begin looking at colleges I will encourage you to reconsider. If you are of a generation where you never really thought about colleges until your junior year I will tell you things have changed significantly. There are several reasons why it is a good idea to start early. First, it will give you plenty of time to research the pros and cons for each institution. Second, you will be able to acclimate to the significant sticker shock you will experience when you see how much tuition, even at state supported colleges, has risen. And third, involving your student in the search can prove motivational. For instance, when you assign them a research project and they enjoy writing about as much as having a root canal, it will be helpful if the college years are not just something nebulous but rather are clothed in visible brick and mortar.

Fourthly, as I mentioned in the previous chapter many students carry several hours of college credit with them into their freshman year of college through CLEP and AP testing. You will want to know if your efforts will be rewarded at specific institutions. And finally college admissions staff pay attention to students and their families that make the effort of a campus visit.

I made frequent use of the Internet when beginning to look at different institutions. Every place has its own Website that provides a means of selling the perfection of their college to anyone who is interested. They are full of helpful information and I encourage you to cyber visit many of them to narrow your search. Other sites such as **www.princetonreview.com** have a wealth of information on most colleges in the U.S. For instance they give reviews by students that include helpful information on the "biggest party school" or "most accessible faculty". Opinions offered by the student body may provide you with information that won't be included in the glossy catalogs or website. Eventually you will want to take the next step and visit some of the campuses. Even if your student is clueless about an area of interest (i.e. a major) you can still gain valuable information regarding the overall environment and attitudes of a college by going through a scheduled visit. If your student does have an area of interest I would encourage you to schedule a visit with a faculty member from that department. They can give you terrific information about what level of competence they expect from incoming students. This can give you time to add or delete something from your curriculum plan. And I will repeat, as noted in my third point above, taking your student to the actual campus will be a visual aid when you try to get them to focus on current tasks for future goals. It may even be helpful for your student to visit local colleges that would never be a serious option, if only to have something for comparison. Once you have visited several campuses, and they have you on their mailing or email list, your student may be invited for a campus visit that may include an overnight stay with ACTUAL COLLEGE STUDENTS! These are usually offered to students in their Junior and Senior year and can also provide helpful information to your student beyond what can be learned in a structured tour. Post visit evaluations of each of these types of excursions are an important part of the process. Ask your student to verbalize their overall impressions. Did the student residences match up to the pictures displayed online? How did the students interact with the professors? Did the students seem generally positive about the institution? How was the food? (I'm not kidding when I tell you that this was a deal breaker on one college visit with my daughter.) How does the tuition rate in comparison to the average financial aid package? If your student has aspirations to participate in college athletics make sure you talk with current athletes in order to evaluate their satisfaction. The same can be said for students who are on Academic or Performance Scholarships. Be nosey, ask lots of graciously probing questions. For instance, "Did you find it hard to balance your practice schedule with your class load?" and "What kind of resources did the school offer to help with those issues?" One of best ways to evaluate an institution is to look at what kind of speakers they invite to speak on campus. You can tell a lot about the philosophical direction of the leadership by looking at their invitation choices. If you are visiting a Secular or State institution, is the lecture list balanced or heavily weighted to only one point of view? If the opportunity arises ask current students what their biggest complaint would be, and then make sure to add a healthy dose of salt.

Remember, for the most part each place you visit will do their best to woo you to their institution. The exception to this rule is the Ivy League Colleges who turn down more than ninety percent of all applicants. In between are colleges that only accept around fifty percent of applicants but still respond graciously to enquiries by prospective students and their families. Another great piece of information on a website like the Princeton Review is the average GPA or test scores of incoming students. This information can be useful in ruling out, or in, any place you are considering.

Once your student has taken the PSAT, SAT or ACT your mailbox will be flooded with invitations to consider different universities. In all likelihood most of these will end up in the trash. Your student may also receive messages and invitations to visit campus through email. They may also be notified of certain times application fees may be waved or they may offer other perks to increase your interest in their college. (You can end up with a ton of T-shirts and water bottles.)

Make sure you enjoy these visits with your student. Never again will you have so many highly motivated people determined to ingratiate themselves. It is a great time to reinforce those critical thinking skills you have tried to teach your student. You have the opportunity to take what you have taught them into a real world situation, only you will be there to help them sort through all the information they will receive. Even if your student decides that college is not for him, these can still be valuable lessons to take into challenging adult situations. College

15

visits can be fun, too soon your student will take those first wobbly steps into adulthood and this can be a first glimpse of that future.

It is also important to assess the Security of the college you are visiting. How many people are on the Security Staff of the institution? Have there been any assaults reported? How secure are the dormitories? Are their Security Staff available to walk students back to cars or dorms after dark? Is the campus well lit? What is their plan for unusual events? Do they notify students by email, text message or other means? It will only take a couple of moments for parents to remember why these questions are relevant.

Finally, resist the urge to regale your student with stories of your college days. In general, despite photographic evidence, your student is probably convinced that you emerged onto the scene just as you are now. They really don't want to think that you might have been young once because that means they may one day be old! This is their experience and no one else has ever been through it. So just sit back and discuss your nostalgic memories with your spouse, they will appreciate them and remember when you could fit into that Leisure Suit.

SUMMARY

START EARLY -THE FRESHMAN YEAR IS NOT TOO EARLY.

USE SEARCH ENGINES TO NARROW YOUR SEARCH.

TALK TO ADMISSION STAFF THAT MAY ATTEND YOUR HOME SCHOOL CONVENTIONS.

WRITE DOWN QUESTIONS YOU OR YOUR STUDENT MAY HAVE BEFORE YOU GO ON A VISIT.

FOR JUNIORS AND SENIORS TRY TO SCHEDULE APPOINTMENTS WITH FACULTY IN YOUR STUDENTS AREA OF INTEREST.

IF YOUR STUDENT IS INTERESTED IN ATHLETICS OR MUSIC MAKE SURE YOU SCHEDULE APPOINTMENTS WITH THOSE DEPARTMENTS.

CHAPTER IV

Transcripts

The Transcript is a document, used by admissions faculty to assess your students' academic accomplishments and fitness for their institution. There are several ways to construct a table to record the data. Several transcript templates are available for purchase or you may develop your own on your personal computer. It is important that you include the following information. First you must identify your school by name. Different states have their own criteria for home schools. Some, like Kansas for instance, basically treat each home school as a private school and families in that state may give their school a name that reflects this ruling. I think that it is a good idea and when you are naming your school consider longevity. "Mom and Dad's Happy Day Academy" may sound good for kindergarten; it will not be nearly as attractive to your seventeen year old. Include the address of your school. For instance:

Constitutional Academy
100 Liberty Avenue
Hometown, Kansas 60311
Student Name- Flowers, Tulips R.
D.O.B. 01/01/1994

TRANSCRIPT

Year	Course	Grade	Credit
2010-2011	English 9	A	1
2010-2011	Algebra I	B	1
2010-2011	Earth Science*	A	1
2010-2011	Health & Wellness	A	.5
2010-1011	Orchestra	A	.5
2010-2011	Bible	A	1

	Credits Earned	GPA
Year	5	3.9
Cumulative	5	3.9

Year	Course	Grade	Credit
2011-2012	English 10	B	1
2011-2012	Algebra II	A	1
2011-2012	Biology*	A	1
2011-2012	Latin I	A	1
2011-2012	Honors U.S. History	A	1

Year	Course	Grade	Credit
2011-2012	Music	A	.5
2011-2012	Orchestra	A	.5
Summer 2012	Geometry	A	1

	Credits Earned	GPA
Year	7	3.83
Cumulative	12	3.86

Year	Course	Grade	Credit
2012-2013	American Literature	A	1
2012-2013	Pre-Calculus	A	1
2012-2013	Chemistry*	A	1
2012-2013	World History	A	1
2012-2013	Latin II	A	1
2012-2013	Orchestra	A	.5
2012-2013	Music	A	.5
2012-2013	Childhood Development	A	1

	Credits Earned	GPA
Year	7	4.0
Cumulative	19	3.91

Year	Course	Grade	Credit
2013-2014	Government/Economics	A	1
2013-2014	World Literature	A	1
2013-2014	Calculus	A	1
2013-2014	Physics	A	1
2013-2014	Honors Psychology	A	1
2013-2014	Journalism	A	1
2013-2014	Music	A	.5
2013-2014	Orchestra	A	.5

	Credits Earned	GPA
Year	7	4.0
Cumulative	25	3.93

*Denotes Lab Component

SAT   June 2013

Critical Reading 640	Math 600	Writing 600

SAT   Sept 2014

Critical Reading 700	Math 650	Writing 650

Graduation Date_____

Official Signature_____

Honors and Awards: Home School Honor Society, National Merit Semifinalist, American Legion Girls State-Governor, First Chair-Violin, Woodwind Conservatory.

This is only one example of a way to set up a transcript. Resist the temptation to elaborate on course descriptions at this point, only the minimum snapshot of your students academic performance is required. The document should be no longer than two pages and make sure the font size is large enough to be read without magnification. If you are listing a course that includes a lab component put an asterisk beside the course and then at the end of the document you may have a table that explains that the asterisk denotes X number of laboratory hours. You may also need to do this if your student finishes what would normally be considered as a year long course in a much shorter period of time. The ending information on this table should total the number of credits and the cumulative GPA. Other information that should be included on this document are the dates and results of your students ACT or SAT test dates and scores. These will not substitute for results sent directly to the college but it is helpful to have the results on the transcript as well. The Document should include a GRADUATION DATE and an OFFICIAL SIGNATURE. You may also include information regarding Awards or Honors but be brief. You can go into more detail on the Leadership Resume. In the fall of your students' senior year the transcript will obviously not be complete. List the courses your student is planning on completing and leave the Graduation Date and Official Signatures blank.

There may be some of you out there who have resisted issuing grades to your student. This presents some difficulty to those who will be looking at the academic record of hundreds of potential students. Even if you have never given your student letter grades you may want to reconsider. Alternate methods of evaluating student performance may have validity but they will require overwhelmed admissions staff to take extra time and effort to decode. Don't give them a reason to place your students' application in the reject pile. Grading is really not all that difficult and some form of it exists in most vocations. You may decide on your own numerical scale for A's and B's etc. If they vary from the 90/100, 80/100 etc. you may want to delineate that information somewhere on the transcript.

You must also include any courses your student has taken from other sources. For instance, if your student has taken any Online Courses they need to be merged onto the Official Transcript. Include any applicable documents within the transcript section. Many homeschooled students are dual enrolled in order to participate in music or sports. You will need to access grades or evaluations from these other sources and include them in the cumulative GPA and Credits. In order to compile an accurate and complete transcript that reflects your students' accomplishments you will have to have some system in place to keep track of each year's courses and grades. I would encourage you to keep this on an ongoing basis so you do not leave out any important content. It is helpful, when you are going on college visits, to have an idea of your students' current GPA and curriculum plan. It is also helpful for your student to understand the relationship between achievement, as it relates to grades, and potential opportunities.

SUMMARY

SET UP YOUR TRANSCRIPT TEMPLATE OR PURCHASE PRE-MADE TEMPLATE.

KEEP AN ONGOING RECORD, UPDATING AS SOON AS YOUR STUDENT HAS FINISHED A COURSE OF STUDY.

KEEP AN ONGOING RECORD OF GRADE POINT AVERAGE.

REVIEW YOUR CURRICULUM PLAN BASED ON YOUR STUDENTS APTITUDE AND INTERESTS.

CHAPTER V

How to figure Grade Point Average.

Imagine for a moment that you work in the admissions office of a university. You have a small desk, a minuscule office, and a window overlooking a campus dumpster. Everyday someone from the mail room deposits stacks of envelopes onto your desk. Inside the envelopes reside the hopes and dreams of many young people. Some of them have a great desire to come to your university, some of them are just going through the motions, and some of them are interested in several universities. Many of the applications will be missing required information. It is your job to sort through this academic debris and either send the applications on for further consideration or contact the applicant for missing information. After you have finished sorting the mail you must then go online and consider all of the applicants that have applied through the "Common Application". Are you feeling their pain? Do you understand that sending them your students' information in the most easily interpreted form can assist all of you? I understand that your student is unique. It can be difficult to objectively assign a value to their academic performance but try you must!

One of the most important pieces of information that is included on your students' high school transcript is the Grade Point Average or GPA. This number is one of many criteria that are used to admit your student into a university and to qualify them for scholarship consideration. By grading your students' performance you are assigning a letter of numerical significance to a particular course of study. For instance, if your student is taking a science course from Apologia, you can make the grade a reflection of daily work and testing. A good rule of thumb is 100-90=A, 89-80=B, 79-70=C ,69-60=D, 59-0=F. You may choose to change those grade ranges but if you do make sure you include a grading key on the official transcript. Courses that are purchased with tests and keys can, if used properly, remove some of the temptation for grade inflation. Having students take courses from Homeschooling Cooperatives or Online will also result in grades from other sources. I found that the hardest items for me to grade were written assignments. I ended up asking a family member who was a retired English teacher to read them and give me an overview and suggestions for improvement before I assigned a grade. Some of you may have avoided grading altogether. I understand that there may be well founded objections to the whole idea of grading as a measure of accomplishment. There are schools that will base admission on review of a student portfolio if they are non-traditional students. If that is the case you will need to talk with the specific institutions to which your student will apply for their requirements. If you have not given your student grades to date but have decided that you will do so, it will make your students high school history easier for colleges to decipher. You can retroactively assign a letter or numerical value to a course of study by reviewing course work. There are certainly problems associated with this and that is why I would encourage you to keep ongoing documentation as your student progresses through secondary school. When assigning a letter grade to a course of study you must decide on a scale. For instance we used a four point scale. An A was given the number 4. A B was given a 3. A C was given a 2 and a D was given a 1. A failed course was assigned a 0. If your student retakes a failed course and achieves a higher grade, then you may remove the earlier score from the transcript. Now you must assign each course a value based on the scope of the course. If you are recording this by semesters, a good rule of thumb is 36 hours rate a value, or credit of 1. As home educators we know that some students will require far less time to complete a course and some will require far more. I would counsel you against trying to weight each course by the actual time spent. It could prove to be a disorienting morass for everyone concerned. After all if Petunia completes her Honors Quantum Physics in one month is that any reason not to give her the two semesters of credit that it would take your Garden Variety Genius. Or if Johnny was distracted by helping Dad run the Combine and took longer to finish his Algebra course he should still only achieve one semester of credit even if he was still working on it in February (I sure hope that boy finishes before its time to plant!). Moving along, you now take the assigned letter grade and multiply it by the credit value. For instance an A is a 4.0. Then multiply it by a value of 1, 4x1=4. The next grade is also an A but the value is only a .5, so you have 4x.5=2. Next, you have a class in which your student achieved a B, or a 3.0. It was also a full semester course so it gets a value of, 3x1=3. Now you take the letter values, 4+2+3=9. This must be divided by the total credit value of the courses, 1+.5+1=2.5. So 9/2.5=3.6. If you are finding this too complicated you can also use one of several GPA calculators available online, my personal favorite is **http://gpacalculator.org**. The advantage of using one of the online sites is that it reduces mathematical errors and can keep an ongoing compilation of grades and GPA.

If your student is taking courses whose content is similar to entry level college courses you may designate those courses as Honors or AP courses. Your student may then choose to take a test at the end of the course for college credit. This may be done through your local government school or by CLEP at local community colleges. There are deadlines and fees for all of these tests which change from year to year so call early in the fall for those sign up times and deadlines. Your students Honors or Advanced Placement courses will give added weight to your students' transcript. Make sure you give your student all the credit that they deserve.

SUMMARY

IF YOU ARE NOT CURRENTLY GRADING YOUR STUDENT RECONSIDER.

DECIDE ON YOUR GRADING SCALE AND NOTE THE SCALE ON YOUR TRANSCRIPT.

RECORD GRADES AFTER YOUR STUDENT COMPLETES EACH COURSE.

USE THE MATHEMATICAL FORMULA ABOVE OR BY USE WWW.GPACALCULATOR.ORG

CHAPTER VI

Documentation of Texts and Curriculum/Letters of Recommendation

You will run into a wide variety of people as you begin the search for the correct school. During this process I had a very disconcerting conversation with an admission official from a large state school. When I related that our student was "Homeschooled" there was a pause followed by throat clearing and the demand that we include a detailed record of what the content of our curriculum included. He then went on to explain that when they received a transcript from a "traditional" school they "knew" what the content of those classes covered. Well you can imagine the effort it took for me to hold my tongue. Was I annoyed? Of course I was. Was I incredulous? Indeed I was! But rather than argue with this ignorant man I decided to take his advice and include a list of the Texts and the Curriculum that we were using, along with an abbreviated listing of the content of those courses. I did not make it part of the Official Transcript but instead included it in the Admission Packet as a separate document. This gives relevant officials the choice of what to consider in their decision. As a Homeschooling family you know that many people are confused about how our children are educated. So I recommend that you keep track of the Texts and Curriculum that you use. Following your Transcript this separate document in your students Admissions Packet should include a list of all of your Math, English, Science, Language and Elective courses. The list should include the titles, authors and perhaps brief list of content. Make sure you include other books that your student has read as part of their education. Done correctly this may run to four or five pages of content that schools can read or ignore at their discretion.

For example:

English: <u>English 9, Grammar, Literature, Writing and </u>, by Dr. Mary Sands, <u>Common Grammar Usage</u>, <u>Adverbs and Prepositions</u>, by Ulysses S. Grant <u>Writing: The Essay</u>, <u>Writing: The Business Letter</u>, <u>Common Grammatical Errors, Rhetorical Excellence</u>. by U. R. Brilliant.

Novels: <u>The Screwtape Letters</u> by C.S. Lewis, Return <u>of the King</u> by J.R. Tolkein, <u>The Count of Montecristo</u> by Alexandre Dumas. Etc. . . .

Letters of Recommendation

Most colleges require letters of recommendation. Many Universities will request letters from your students' teachers. Obviously a letter from the students' parent waxing eloquent on juniors attributes would be silly. As Homeschooling students become more sought after I expect this will change but that doesn't help you here and now. This is when you must think outside the box. "Teacher" doesn't have to mean only the local public school employees. It can also mean your students Violin or Piano teacher. After all what they really want to see reflected on paper is your students attitude towards hard work and persistence. A letter from your Pastor can reflect on your students' character. A letter from an employer can give insight into work and attendance habits, learning style and ability to work with others.

Make sure when you request a letter of recommendation that you put your request in writing and include the following: an idea about when you will need the completed letter, the focus of the letter (academic, character, work habits etc.) permission to photo copy the letter for use on multiple applications. Be considerate of the time and effort it takes for your pastor or coach to accommodate your request. They may get many requests for similar letters and it is unreasonable for you to expect an instant response. If, after multiple gentle reminders you still do not have a letter from a piano teacher etc. you may want to consider moving on. Some people are just not capable of writing a good reference letter in a timely manner. It has been my experience that the product that they produce may not actually be something you will want to use. Some institutions will want the letter mailed directly to their office from the writer. This is actually quite correct and well within the norm. However as a practical matter, if your student is going to be applying to multiple institutions the ability to photo copy and include the same letter in several packets can simplify the process. Make sure the letter writer includes a contact number so that the institution can make further inquiries. Believe it or not people have been known to fabricate these documents so contact information on the letter confirms that you are fine with them verifying the existence of the letter writer.

Example:

10/10/2013

Dr. Earnest Cello
Woodwind Conservatory
1011 Glistening Glenn Lane.
Hometown, Kansas 60011

Magna Carta University
800 Creekside Blvd.
Last Hope Virginia 10039

Dear Sirs:

I am writing on behalf of my student, Tulip R. Flowers, and it is a delight to do so! She is the kind of student that rarely comes into the life of an instructor such as myself. She is an exceptionally talented Violinist and has been First Chair in our Orchestra for the last two years. Indeed my only regret is that her matriculation will result in the loss of her leadership. Unlike many young people who are musically gifted, she is also humble, open to instruction, and an exceptionally hard worker. The most remarkable characteristic of my young student is her passion to share her love of the violin with the less fortunate in our community. She has begun a program to introduce stringed instruments to students from our immigrant community and has paired those youngsters with instruments and instructors. She has led many fund raising events to supplement the costs of this program. She has done this while continuing to pursue a rigorous academic program.

As you can see, this is an extraordinary young woman and I give her my highest recommendation as a musician, student, and as compassionate young woman. She is that rarest of person, one who is willing to give of herself to make a difference in the lives of others.

If you are able to persuade this young woman to attend your University you will be fortunate indeed! Please feel free to contact me at 800-555-5555.

Sincerely yours,

Dr. Earnest Cello

SUMMARY

MAINTAIN RECORDS AND DOCUMENTS INCLUDING:

TRANSCRIPT/GPA

LIST OF TEXTS AND CURRICULUM

LETTERS OF REFERENCE

COURSES AND GRADES FROM OTHER SOURCES

CHAPTER VII

Leadership/Service Resume

Many colleges and universities ask students competing for admission or scholarships to submit a summary of activities that the student has initiated during their high school years. They are interested in what your student has participated in outside their academic endeavors. Projects should show the strengths of character, talents and the initiative of your student. I strongly urge you to begin thinking about your students' gifts and interests early in their high school experience. Be creative and brainstorm ideas that engage your students' passions. Are they gifted athletically? Maybe they can start a program working with young athletes in T-ball or swimming. If they are gifted in some other area you may help your student offer a service project to their church or community. Do they have a heart for the elderly; perhaps they can start an Adopt an Elder program at a local Nursing Home. Do you live on a farm? You may be able to participate in leadership roles in 4-H or FFA. Or maybe your student could initiate a program of farm visits for city kids. Perhaps they can teach a "Farm Safety" class. The idea can be as varied as your students' circumstances and abilities. The important thing is for your student to think beyond academics. They should be integral in the planning and follow through of the project. It is important that your student plan the activity from initial idea to its practical application. For instance their plan may follow this example:

1. Assess the needs and goals of your project. (Are there children in your community that would benefit from a summer activity?)

2. Does your student possess, or can they develop, the ability to meet this need, either by themselves, or with the help of other interested students?

3. Can your student gather the resources to meet that need?

4. Make a list of the things they will need to do to make the project run smoothly. Itemize any materials you may need. Will you need the financial support of others? Depending on the project, you may be able to receive help from local organizations already involved in your area of interest. (For instance the local American Legion Auxiliary gave my daughter assistance when she presented a project for care packages for soldiers).

5. Set up a Timeline for accomplishing these things. When do you want the project to start? Do you need to gain permission or assistance in order to move forward with your plan? If so, you may need to present a board or supervisor with an outline of your plan and its goals. Is your Timeline dependent on other people's schedule? If so, you will need to coordinate with everyone involved. Get a notebook to keep track of every participant's contact information and schedule. Make a task list of things that need to be done and check them off as you go. Learn to delegate. Give parts of your project to other participants but don't forget to follow up and make sure all parts are progressing in a timely manner. Depending on the complexity and length of your project you may need to do this on an ongoing basis.

6. Initiate the project. Make sure the target group knows about your project. This may include phone calls, flyers, email and even newspapers or community message boards. The day before the start of your project make sure you have confirmed all of your materials and personnel are in place. Go through your "What ifs?" For instance what if twenty more four year olds show up for your class than you had planned? Something you didn't anticipate will happen! Think through possible scenarios and how you will respond. Don't forget

to enjoy! Remind your student that they chose this project because they were truly interested.

7. After completion, assess the project for both its strengths and failures; document what you have learned from the process. Did you meet your goals? As stated in number 6 every project has its surprises. Some of them are great and some not so great. The important thing for your student is that they honestly assess the project and are able to make any changes to improve or correct the process. It is very important that the people reading your students Service/Leadership Resume recognize that your student has the ability to recognize deficiencies and make changes.

8. Keep any feedback you receive from the participants for documentation purposes. For instance, thank you notes from parents, or any feedback you receive from the participants. Take pictures of the participants during the activity. You will need to obtain permission for other people's children to appear in photos if you plan to include them in any publication. If you are lucky enough to get your project featured in a local paper then you can include those articles in your students' portfolio. So, call the paper, they are usually interested in these types of projects, and your students' effort will be documented by an outside source.

Having trouble thinking of a project? You may want to begin with things with which your family is already involved. Is there a church activity that your student can take to the next level by their own initiative? Is there something in which your student is already accomplished or interested that has revealed an unmet need? For instance are you aware of other students who could benefit from one to one tutoring in math or reading? Are there people in your community who could use assistance with yard work or errands? Perhaps your student could organize a system that assists with those needs. Does your student have an interest in politics? Even in an off year there are usually lots of tasks to be done and you don't have to be old enough to vote to do it! Learning to recognize need and breaking down solutions into manageable items are skills that every citizen needs. Every one of us is faced daily with accomplishing work and solving problems. During the college interview your student may be asked how they have accomplished problem solving in the past. Like most things "practice makes perfect". The more times they have participated in this process, the easier it will be for them to talk about it in an essay or interview.

9. Make sure your student acknowledges everyone who helped with their project. They can either print "Certificates of Participation" on your personal computer or better yet write letters to key participants. If the participants are students they can then use these to document their admission efforts, and if they are adult participants it is correct to thank them in writing. Example:

Service Resume

Miss Tulips R. Flowers

To Serve: To Recognize and Meet the Needs of Others.

Project: Mathematics Mentors. Math Mentors is an organization that was begun by local educators in our Homeschooling Association. This organization pairs student who are struggling with their math curriculum with older students who have mastered those mathematical functions. Having participated in this program first as a student and then as a tutor I was able to see how effective peer mentoring can be. My first mentor helped me conquer my math anxiety. Once I was confident of my own skills I wanted to share my new found love of math with other struggling students. I have now mentored six fellow students. Four of these students were part of the Homeschooling Community but I have also been asked to mentor students in our local public school. I hope to continue to participate in a similar program throughout my college years. Through my participation in this program I learned to overcome my fears and pass on my math confidence to others.

Project: Botswanian Resettlement Project. I became involved, along with my family, in our churches effort to resettle refugees from the nation of Botswana. Our churches youth group gathered household goods and basic food items to help resettle four families totaling twenty eight people. Along with collecting these items we were able to adopt an individual family and help them work through the "culture shock" of arriving in a Midwestern state in January. As president of my youth group I organized the drive to collect the needed items and distribute them to each family. I learned to make lots of lists and delegate tasks among my fellow students. This operation was so rewarding that I am sure that I have made friend that will last a lifetime. It also made me very aware of how blessed we truly are in America.

Project: Bows for Botswanians. During my families participation in our churches resettlement project I became aware of several youngsters interest in our church orchestra. Although this is far different from traditional African music I found many of my young friends requesting instruction. Through the outreach ministry of our church we were able to raise funds to rent or buy several instruments and pair eager young students with willing instructors. I followed up with each student and spent time instructing them on instrument care and storage. Watching as their skills and love of music increased was a great experience. Before I leave this project to attend college, I hope to train another Musician/ Leader to carry on the program.

SUMMARY

START ENCOURAGING YOUR STUDENT TO THINK OF POTENTIAL PROJECTS EARLY.

HELP YOUR STUDENT PLAN THEIR PROJECT AND KEEP ON A SCHEDULE.

HELP YOUR STUDENT KEEP A RECORD OF ACTIVITIES.

ASSESS YOUR FAMILY AND COMMUNITY FOR POSSIBLE PROJECTS.

CONSIDER LINKING WITH CURRENT ORGANIZATIONS FOR FINANCIAL AND OTHER ASSISTANCE.

ASSESS THE PROJECT AFTER COMPLETION, INCLUDE INFORMATION ON BOTH POSITIVE AND NEGATIVE RESULTS.

TEACH YOUR STUDENT TO BREAK DOWN PROBLEMS INTO MANAGEABLE PORTIONS.

PICK PROJECTS IN WHICH YOUR STUDENT HAS A GENUINE INTEREST.

CHAPTER VIII

Interviews

Once your student has sent in all of the required documents they may receive a request from the university for an interview. Some schools require an interview before they will issue a decision on admission. One of the schools which we were considering had several off campus events where interviews were conducted. Others will require that you travel to their campus at a time of their choosing. One university that offered our student a presidential scholarship also offered to pay the expenses for her to attend the interview. The interview arrangements are as varied as the school.

When preparing for the interviews use the same advice given to job applicants. Dress appropriately, jeans and T-shirts may be fine for a campus visit but not for an interview. For young men a jacket and tie should be worn. Hair should be well groomed and off your face. Make sure you are showered and clean, and that includes fingernails! For young women I would encourage modest business casual. In other words your hair should be off the face. Make up, if worn, should be simple and natural looking. Avoid shirts that may show cleavage and skirts that slide up when sitting. These things will distract and detract from the important things you may want to communicate. Avoid clothing that is too tight. If finances are an issue I recommend that you seek out Consignment Stores in your area, most carry an assortment of both men's and women's business clothing. Make sure that the shoes you wear not only match but are comfortable. Any visit to a campus is going to require walking. Blisters can be very distracting! During the interview make sure you smile and make eye contact. They are going to want to know how you found out about their university and why you are interested in attending. Be honest! If you really want to attend a school close to the coast so that you can continue to rescue baby sea urchins, let them know. If they have an amazing Study Abroad program and you want to become proficient in Manchurian, they will want to know that too. In some ways you are interviewing them, so it is appropriate to ask questions. Let them know what interests and assets you can bring to their campus and what kind of student and person you really are! If the school with which you are interviewing is your first choice let them know! If it is only one of many in which you are equally interested you can let them know that too! The school may be shopping for the right blend of students but you are also shopping for the college that gives you the best overall fit. Another type of interview that your student may experience is one involving scholarship competitions. After your student has been accepted by a university they may be invited to apply for Merit Based Scholarships. This may require another written application including an essay or answers to specific questions. These scholarships are usually time sensitive. In other words if all applications and documents need to be postmarked by December 1st, don't expect them to accept yours marked December the 6th. These invitations are usually issued in response to GPA, Transcript and SAT or ACT scores. If your student has applied to and been accepted by several places you may find that they have conflicting invitations. For instance in January of my students' senior year, several invitations were received for the same dates in February. We had to sit down and prioritize based on which schools she was most interested in attending. Some places will offer more than one date for their competitions but many don't. This is also a winnowing procedure for the colleges to see just who is really interested and motivated enough to make the effort to attend. In general a scholarship day will involve informational meetings for both the student and the parents. Your student may be asked to write an impromptu essay as well as be interviewed by faculty. In these interviews faculty will attempt to probe the breadth and depth of your students' interest in current events, conflicts and their worldview. There may be an opening for your student to talk about their own experiences and how those experiences enriched or changed them. Students who have been home schooled may well have a significant advantage in this type of situation because they have not been imprisoned for eight hour a day with other teenagers. Instead they may have been exposed to a wide variety of ages and can converse coherently with adults and other alien life forms. If however, your student has a great deal of anxiety or is shy you may want to consider some form of practice before the actual interview. They could start out practicing with you or your spouse and then move on to another adult with whom they are comfortable, and lastly practice with people who are less familiar such as an adult friend from church. Don't use the same questions at every practice session because this really isn't about having the "right" answers. Instead the goal should be to reduce your students "game day" anxiety by working through unfamiliar situations. You want your students' real personhood to shine through not rote answers to rote questions. For instance, at one scholarship day that we attended, my daughter was walking across campus with several students and faculty. They were having a lively discussion and my daughter proceeded to walk right into a decorative lamp post, the professor stopped and asked if she was ok, she started laughing and told him "Don't worry, things like this happen to me all the time!". I'm not recommending this as an ice breaker but sometimes how you respond to the unexpected can be just as informative as all the preparation in the world.

SUMMARY

PREPARING FOR INTERVIEW SHOULD INCLUDE:

MAKING SURE YOUR APPEARANCE IS NOT DISTRACTING.

MALE STUDENTS SHOULD, MINIMIZE FACIAL HAIR, REMOVE EARRINGS, MAKE SURE HAIR IS OFF THE FACE AND WELL GROOMED. CONSIDER WEARING A WELL FITTING JACKET, SHIRT AND TIE. WEAR COMFORTABLE BUT MATCHING SHOES. MAKE SURE YOUR NAILS ARE SHORT AND CLEAN.

FEMALE STUDENTS SHOULD, MINIMIZE MAKEUP AND EARRINGS. HAIR SHOULD BE WELL GROOMED AND OFF THE FACE. REVIEW YOUR WARDROBE FOR APPROPRIATE BUSINESS CASUAL CLOTHING. THESE SHOULD BE WELL FITTING BUT NOT TIGHT! DO NOT WEAR ANYTHING THAT IS LOW CUT OR IN THE CASE OF SKIRTS SLIDE UP WHEN SITTING.

CONSIDER SHOPPING SPECIFICALLY FOR AN INTERVIEW IF YOU DO NOT HAVE APPROPRIATE CLOTHING. REMEMBER CONSIGNMENT STORES CAN BE GREAT SOURCES FOR INEXPENSIVE BUSINESS CLOTHING.

IF YOUR STUDENT IS RETICENT CONSIDER PRACTICING.

MAKE EYE CONTACT WITH THE INTERVIEWER AND REMEMBER TO SMILE.

DON'T BE DISCOURAGED IF YOU DON'T FEEL YOU DID YOUR BEST, FINDING THE RIGHT FIT MAY NOT HAPPEN AT THE FIRST INTERVIEW.

CHAPTER IX

Making a decision

During the summer following your students' junior year you should have narrowed your search to a handful of colleges. After the search has been narrowed you will want to review the specific entrance requirement for those colleges to make sure you will have all of the required courses. There is still time to include specific courses in your students' senior year. You will also want to verify exactly which AP or CLEP credits each institution will accept. You may consider schools who accept the "Common Application" as they often waive fees if applications are completed Online.

Now is the time to consider another visit to your top two or three schools. October is a popular month for student visits that include an overnight stay in the dormitory. At some point you and your student need to sit down and assess your overall impressions and start to eliminate schools in which you are no longer interested. Do not rule out private colleges just because their tuition prices may be considerably higher than state run institution. After you have submitted your FAFSA report you will receive a Student Aide offer from colleges to which your student has been accepted. You will need to have narrowed your search so that those colleges can each receive a report from FAFSA and complete your offer. Scholarship offers may be received separately but will then be included on the Student Aide offer.

Don't be discouraged by doors that are shut due to non-admission or unsatisfactory financial aid packages. This is a winnowing process whose goal is to connect your student with the college that will allow them to thrive. Once your student has made a decision I would encourage them to notify all of the colleges to which they have been accepted. Many students are on "Wait Lists" and can then be moved up and possibly accepted. In addition, any colleges that have offered your student a scholarship should be informed of their decision at the first opportunity. Those funds may then be reallocated to other deserving students.

SUMMARY

BEFORE THE SENIOR YEAR: NARROW YOUR CHOICES TO A HANDFULL OF SCHOOLS.

RE-VISIT YOUR TOP CHOICES.

CONSIDER ATTENDING AN OVERNIGHT VISIT.

AFTER COMPLETION OF FAFSA, CONSIDER ALL OF YOUR CHOICES BY COMPARING COST AND FINANCIAL AIDE PACKAGES.

CONSIDER THE OVER ALL FIT OF YOUR FINALISTS.

NOTIFY ALL OF THE FINAL COLLEGES OF YOUR DECISION.

CHAPTER X

Timeline

Before the Freshman Year

_ Keep a record of any High School level courses that your student has already taken.

_ Plan the sequence of the Science/ Lab courses for your student.

_ Plan the sequence of Mathematics courses for your student.

_ Plan the Sequence of English Courses, including Literature, Grammar, Vocabulary and Journalism.

_ Review potential Foreign Language courses.

_ Evaluate your students' abilities and interests for potential Service/ Leadership projects.

Freshman Year

Review College Preparatory Curriculum Choices, select:

_ A Science Course with a Laboratory component (i.e. Earth, General Science or Biology)

_Algebra I (Geometry or Algebra II if Algebra I has already been taken)

_World or U.S. History

_Freshman English (Including Literature, Vocabulary, Grammar, Writing Proficiency)

_Foreign Language

_Electives (Bible, Music, Art, Physical Education etc.)

Keep an ongoing record of all Novels, Texts, Articles including Titles, Authors and Class Content.

Update entries on your Official Transcript, review GPA each semester.

Assess your students' progress and interests and make necessary adjustments.

Sophomore Year

_Science with a Laboratory Component (Biology/ Chemistry)

_Algebra II or Geometry

_World or U.S. History

_English (American Literature, Writing, etc.)

_Foreign Language II

_Electives

_Consider Advanced Placement/Honors Classes

August- Consider registering to take a "practice" PSAT tests in September

January- Contact your local school or go online to register for AP testing dates.

May/June -Update your students' records and GPA.

June through August after your students' sophomore year:

_Consider enrolling your student in a PSAT preparatory class.

-Register your student for the PSAT test.

_Encourage your student to take Pre-Calculus over the summer to improve PSAT performance.

_Put Nineteenth Century Literature on your Summer Reading List.

Junior Year

_September/October- Take PSAT test

_Schedule College trips

_Review Students Service/Leadership Projects

_October/November- Review your Students PSAT score and make curriculum adjustments as needed.

_Schedule your student for ACT or SAT tests.

_Continue with your College Preparatory Courses.

   _Science (Chemistry, Physics)

   _Algebra II, Geometry, or Pre-calculus

   _U.S. Government/ Economics

   _English

   _Additional Language

   _Electives

   _Consider AP/Honors classes

June-August after your Junior Year

_Review potential college choices.

_Continue Service/Leadership Projects.

_Gather documents for Admission Packet.

_Begin to fill out college applications.

Senior Year

_August-October: Finish filling out College Applications. Include finished Admission Packet in mailing. Double check that all submissions include required documents, payment, etc.

_MAKE SURE YOUR ADMISSION PACKET INCLUDES THE FOLLOWING:

> _Cover Letter
>
> _Official Transcript
>
> _Summary of Texts & Curriculum
>
> _Supporting documentation (Online classes, Home School Co-ops etc.)
>
> _Leadership/ Service Resume
>
> _Letters of Recommendation

_Prioritize your College Choices.

_Schedule college visits with Coaches, Music and Performance Arts Departments.

_Schedule additional ACT/SAT tests (consider enrolling in a test prep class).

SENIOR YEAR CURRICULUM- Finish Strong!

_Science (Physics/ AP Biology, Chemistry)

_Mathematics

_U.S. Government/ Economics (if not taken earlier)

_Literature (Emphasize writing competency)

_Additional Language

_Honors/AP History

_Electives

NOVEMBER

_Double check dates for Scholarship applications.

_Make sure all required documents are mailed by the designated deadline.

JANUARY

_If invited, decide which scholarship days your student will attend. RSVP!

_Fill out your Federal Application for Student Aid, or FAFSA.

FEBRUARY

_Review wardrobe for appropriate "Business Casual" clothing for interviews.

_Attend your selected Scholarship Days. Enjoy yourself and let your personality shine through!

MARCH/APRIL

_Review your FAFSA report along with your EFC (Expected Family Contribution).

_Review all offers from your finalists.

MAY

_Respond to all offers as soon as possible by phone, email and or mail.

_GRADUATE (Eat your cake; toss your mortar board, Carpe Diem!)

JUNE-AUGUST

_Schedule your "Freshman Orientation".

_Be sure to contact your roommate. (You'll want to coordinate who brings the mini fridge etc.)

_Pack (And don't forget to clean your room!)

CONCLUSION

At the start of this book I told you that my goal was to walk you through the search for a college, and the creation of a packet of information that your student can submit to colleges for admission consideration. The packet that we developed included the following: A cover letter written by our student to colleges listing the things she was looking for in a school, the transcript, supporting documents, list of Tests and Curriculum, and Letters of Recommendation. I suggest that you consider taking your documents to a printer and have a cover applied. This will keep your documents together and give it a more polished appearance.

In wrapping up this book I would like to say something about academic integrity. Out there, in the world of traditional schooling, the awareness of academic dishonesty and grade inflation is oft discussed. Computer programs have been developed to discover plagiarism or the purchasing of written material. It is an insidious problem and one to which Homeschoolers have no immunity. I ask you to hold yourselves to the highest of standards. Do not give your students grades they do not deserve. Likewise, do not deflate their grades but strive honestly to assess their efforts. I have heard of parents who write their students admission essays or hire other students to do so. Aside from the fact that this is fraudulent, in the end it will damage your student. It not only teaches them to behave dishonestly to achieve a desired outcome but it also tells them that you do not believe them competent or capable. In the end you will not be able to continue to provide them with this crutch. How much better it would be to put in the effort to improve your students writing skills. Then you can note with pride their improvement. Deny yourself and your student the temporary relief of crossing a task off of a long list. Instead insist on promoting your students efforts. It will provide the long term reward of developing your students' confidence and personal integrity.

APPENDIX

Websites

SAT/PSAT: www.Collegeboard.com

ACT: www.act.org

FAFSA: www.fafsa.ed.gov

College Search websites: www.Princetonreview.com
www.collegeboard.com

Testing Prep: www.barronstestprep.com
www.princetonreview.com
www.ivyinsiders.com

Advanced Placement Testing: www.collegeboard.com/student/testing/
AP/about.html

College Level Examination Program: www.collegeboard.com/student/
testing/clep/about.html

- NOTES ON COLLEGE VISITS
  - o NAME OF COLLEGE

  - o TUITION/ROOM AND BOARD

  - o HOUSING CHOICES

  - o CAFETERIA QUALITY (1-10, 1 AWFUL-10 GREAT!)

  - o QUESTIONS FOR ADMISSION STAFF.

  - o SECURITY ASSESSMENT

NOTES

NOTES

- NOTES ON COLLEGE VISITS
  - o NAME OF COLLEGE

  - o TUITION/ROOM AND BOARD

  - o HOUSING CHOICES

  - o CAFETERIA QUALITY (1-10, 1 AWFUL-10 GREAT!)

  - o QUESTIONS FOR ADMISSION STAFF.

  - o SECURITY ASSESSMENT

NOTES

NOTES

- NOTES ON COLLEGE VISITS

    o NAME OF COLLEGE

    o TUITION/ROOM AND BOARD

    o HOUSING CHOICES

    o CAFETERIA QUALITY (1-10, 1 AWFUL-10 GREAT!)

    o QUESTIONS FOR ADMISSION STAFF.

    o SECURITY ASSESSMENT

NOTES

NOTES

- NOTES ON COLLEGE VISITS

    o NAME OF COLLEGE

    o TUITION/ROOM AND BOARD

    o HOUSING CHOICES

    o CAFETERIA QUALITY (1-10, 1 AWFUL-10 GREAT!)

    o QUESTIONS FOR ADMISSION STAFF.

    o SECURITY ASSESSMENT

NOTES

NOTES

- NOTES ON COLLEGE VISITS
    - o NAME OF COLLEGE

    - o TUITION/ROOM AND BOARD

    - o HOUSING CHOICES

    - o CAFETERIA QUALITY (1-10, 1 AWFUL-10 GREAT!)

    - o QUESTIONS FOR ADMISSION STAFF.

    - o SECURITY ASSESSMENT

NOTES

NOTES

LaVergne, TN USA
26 April 2010
180614LV00002B/33/P

9 781615 070855